Letters to God

Quiet Moments in Written Conversation with God

2026

By
Steve Chianos

A Simple Prayer

"My prayers are with you." "I'll keep you in my prayers."

We all say those words so easily, but how often do we actually pray? How often do we actually take time to sit in quiet contemplation and ask the Lord to help those we said we would keep in our prayers?

Okay, before you start sending me messages telling me about your daily devotions, I know, a lot of people pray every day. They bow their heads before meals and at least once a day in communion with God.

But for a lot of us, praying is a hard thing to do. We sit down to commune with the Lord the words just aren't there. Talking to God, is intimidating and we don't know how to start.

I've struggled with with my faith most of my life, so it shouldn't come as a surprise to me that I'm one of the latter.

Then, one day I'm sitting in church listening to our pastor deliver a message on prayer. It was part of a series of messages about prayer, but this one struck home for me. While I was listening, something he said clicked.

Prayers don't have to be grand.

Prayers don't have to be official.

<u>Payers can be simple.</u>

"Lord, please help me."

"Lord, thank you for loving me."

"Lord, I'm lost and need your guidance."

You don't have to explain what's in your heart in detail, because He already knows. The important part is to take a little time to commune with God and acknowledge that you welcome Him into your heart.

I don't know why it clicked, but it did, and a song lyric popped into my head.

"Lord, please help me help my stupid self." ~ Watching You by Rodney Atkins

I wish I could say this was unusual, but that's just how my brain works. I don't understand why it works this way, so please don't ask.

My mind made a couple more leaps about adding daily, or at least regular prayer to my life. I wanted a way to pray that wasn't intimidating. Yes, praying to the Creator is intimidating. Who am I to ask for the attention of the Creator of everything.

My mind returned to Rodney Atkins' song.

"He closed his little eyes, folded his little hands, spoke to God like he was talkin' to a friend." ~ *Watching You by Rodney Atkins*

Looking at those lyrics in the context of my Pastor's message gave me a new perspective on prayer.

Prayer doesn't need to be formal. It doesn't need to be 'official words' taken from the scripture. Prayer could be as simple as talking with God like I'm talking with a friend.

Since it's not going to be the same give and take as talking with a friend, clearly God's not going to respond to your thoughts with his own, it can still be that simple.

A Letter to God

This left me with two questions.

First, can I find a way to add regular prayer to my life that is meaningful to me.

Second, if I'm talking to a friend and they aren't going to hold up their side of the conversation in real time, can I really call it talking to a friend?

Thinking about the second question, led me to an answer for the first.

Talking with the Lord isn't the same as sitting in a coffee shop talking to a friend. The conversation isn't going to have the same exchange of thoughts that a regular conversation does. Don't get me wrong, it isn't that God isn't listening, He is. And it isn't that He won't respond, to your prayer, He will, but we just don't always realize when He's responding.

Talking to God is more like sending a friend a letter or an email. You write down what's on your mind and in your heart and send it to them and then you wait for a response.

When you talk with God like you're talking with a friend, you tell Him what's in your heart and send it out to him as a prayer. He'll respond in His own way in His own time. You may not always recognize His response, but He will respond.

Writing letters to God. What an easy way to pray to God on a regular basis.

So I decided to create a devotional to help make writing letters to God a regular part of life. Yes, I didn't say daily devotional. I didn't say daily because this edition of Letters to God is intended to be a place to start and to work your way up to a daily devotional. That edition of Letters to God will come out soon.

Writing Your Letters to God

Why isn't Letters to god a daily devotional? Because starting a habit of praying to God everyday is little intimidating. For that reason, with the exception of Christmas and Easter, I've designed this devotional to be flexible. You can start building a habit of writing our letters to God a little at a time. Maybe 3 or 4 a week.

During Christmas and Easter, I think it's important to take a little extra time to reflect on your faith and contemplate your relationship with the Lord. For that reason, Letters to God encourages you to write a Letter to God every day during the weeks leading up to Christmas and Easter.

I know it can be hard to start. Remember when you sit down to write your letters that you're talking to a friend. If you don't have anything in mind to pray about, start with gratitude. Think about something that you have to be thankful for and begin your letter with that.

If starting with gratitude every day doesn't feel right, tell the Lord about your day, or the day ahead of you. Tell Him about your failures and successes. Thank Him for your successes and ask Him to help you carry the burden of your failures. Ask Him to help you learn from from your failures and be humble in your success.

If you're looking for a little inspiration, the top of every page has a Bible verse along with a prompt to think about. Read the verse and think about it while you're writing your letter.

I know that reading the bible can be hard to understand and it's even harder when the verses are read on their own with out the surrounding context. I made sure to include the book and chapter with each verse so you can take a few minutes to look one up to get more context before writing your letter.

Bottom line, there is no right or wrong way to write your letters to God. If your happy, tell Him. If you're hurting, tell Him. If you have a loved one in need, tell Him. You don't have to go into great detail, He already knows. He knows what's in your heart. Write to Him and let Him celebrate by your side. Write to Him and let Him help shoulder the burdens you carry.

Talk to God like you're talking to a friend. And when you're ready for more, look for my daily devotional; Letters to God: 365 Letters of Faith, Hope and Gratitude.

Jeremiah 29:12

"Then you will call on me and come and pray to me, and I will

listen to you."

Call on God and listen to hear his promise.

Let me help you get started.

Dear Lord,

It normally take time at the end of the day to read Your Word and think about what I've read. But today is big day for me and I wanted to tell you about it before I leave.

I'm meeting with a client today to talk about merging our businesses. We have a lot of overlap and I think we both would benefit from sharing our resources.

I'm worried though that I may be rushing into this merger because I'm getting tired of working alone.

Please guide my path so that I make the right choices today.

Steve

Remember, you don't have to go into a lot of detail. He already knows. If it helps, keep it simple and talk to Him like you're talking to a friend.

The Name of Jesus

Luke 2:21

"When eight days were fulfilled for the circumcision of the child, his name was called Jesus, which was given by the angel before he was conceived in the womb."

What does the name "Jesus mean to you personally? Thank Him for the ways He has rescued and carried you.

January 1

The Word was God

John 1:1-2

"In the beginning was the Word, and the Word was with God, and the Word was God. He was in the beginning with God."

What part of God's unchanging nature brings you comfort today? Ask him for deeper trust in His eternal character.

January 2

The True Light

John 1:9

"The true light that enlightens everyone was coming into the world."

Where do you need Jesus to bring clarity or direction? Ask Him to illuminate your next step.

January 3

Born King of the Jews

Matthew 2:2

"'Where is he who is born King of the Jews? For we saw his star in the east, and have come to worship him.'"

Unlike the Wise men, we don't have to search for Jesus, he is knocking at the door waiting for you to invite him in. Write to him today and invite him into your home.

January 4

They Rejoiced with Great Joy

Matthew 2:10

"When they saw the star, they rejoiced with exceedingly great joy."

Where has God given you joy recently? Spend a few moments thanking Him for the gifts that brighten your path.

January 5

We Have Come to Worship Him (Epiphany)

Matthew 2:11

"They came into the house and saw the young child with Mary, his mother, and they fell down and worshiped him… they presented to him gifts: gold, frankincense, and myrrh."

What gift can you offer Jesus today—your time, trust, worship, or obedience? Write to him today with an open heart and talk to him about the gift of his presence in your life..

January 6

Jeremiah 29:12

"Then you will call on me and come and pray to me, and I will listen to you."

Write your letter knowing that God is listening — tell him what matters most to you today.

January

Matthew 6:5–6

"Whenever you pray, don't be like the hypocrites, for they love to stand and pray in the synagogues and on the street corners to be seen by men. Most certainly I tell you, they have their reward. But whenever you pray, go into your inner room, close the door, and pray to your Father who is in secret; and your Father who sees in secret will reward you."

Consider setting aside a little space in your home where you can sit quietly every day to write your letter to God.

January

Matthew 6:9–13

"After this manner therefore pray: 'Our Father who is in heaven, hallowed be your name. Your kingdom come. Your will be done in earth, as it is in heaven. Give us this day our daily bread. And forgive us our debts, as we forgive our debtors. And lead us not into temptation, but deliver us from evil.' "

Reflect on the lord prayer and consider someone you have been denying forgiveness. Ask the Lord to help you lighten your heart by forgiving that person. Especially if you are the one you've been denying forgiveness.

January

Matthew 7:7

"Ask, and it will be given to you; seek, and you will find; knock, and it will be opened to you."

Ask God for one specific need right now and listen for His guidance.

January

Matthew 21:22

"And all things, whatever you ask in prayer, believing, you will receive."

It isn't enough to simply write to your friend. You must have faith that your friend will receive your letter and read it. He will.

January

Matthew 26:41

"Watch and pray, that you will not enter into temptation. The spirit indeed is willing, but the flesh is weak."

Ask God for vigilance and strength where you are vulnerable.

January

Mark 11:24–25

"Therefore I tell you, whatever things you ask when you pray, believe that you receive them, and you will have them. And whenever you stand praying, forgive, if you have anything against anyone; that your Father also who is in heaven may forgive you your trespasses."

Bring a need and a relationship before God—write and ask for both provision and for forgiveness.

January

Luke 11:1–4

"Now Jesus was praying in a certain place, and when he finished, one of his disciples said to him, 'Lord, teach us to pray, as John also taught his disciples.' He said to them, 'When you pray, say: Father, hallowed be your name. Your kingdom come. Give us each day our daily bread. Forgive us our sins, for we also forgive everyone who is indebted to us. And lead us not into temptation.'"

Ask the Lord to teach you to pray with simplicity and dependence.

January

Luke 18:1

"He also told them a parable to the effect that they ought always to pray and not to lose heart."

Make a habit of writing your letters—resolve to keep writing even if answers aren't immediately apparent.

January

Luke 21:36

"But keep watching at all times, and pray that you may be counted worthy to escape all these things that will come to pass, and to stand before the Son of Man."

Write to Jesus about the things in your live that are tempting you to stray from your faith. Ask him to give you the strength to walk the path the Lord has planned for you.

January

Luke 22:40

"When he had come to the place, he said to them, 'Pray that you may not enter into temptation.'"

Name a present temptation and ask God for deliverance.

January

Luke 22:32

"But I have prayed for you, that your faith should not fail. And when you have turned again, strengthen your brothers."

Thank Jesus for praying for you, and ask Him to strengthen you to help others in their faith.

February

John 14:13–14

"Whatever you will ask in my name, that will I do, that the Father may be glorified in the Son. If you will ask anything in my name, I will do it."

Write to Jesus and tell him about a moment in your life when you saw Gods glory shine.

February

John 14:27

"Peace I leave with you. My peace I give to you. I don't give to you as the world gives. Don't let your heart be troubled, neither let it be fearful."

Ask God to fill you with His peace where anxiety has crept in.

February

John 15:7

"If you abide in me, and my words abide in you, you will ask whatever you will, and it will be done for you."

Ask God to help you abide in Christ that your prayers reflect his will.

February

John 16:24

"Until now you have asked nothing in my name. Ask, and you will receive, that your joy may be made full."

Write to God and trust that he will answer in his own way. Let your faith fill you with joy.

February

Acts 2:42

"They continued steadfastly in the apostles' teaching and fellowship, in the breaking of bread, and in prayers."

Ask God to help you find a deeper devotion to Scripture, fellowship, and prayer in your community.

February

Acts 3:1

"Now Peter and John were going up to the temple at the hour of prayer, the ninth hour."

Consider setting aside a regular time for prayer every day.

February

Acts 6:4

"But we will give ourselves continually to prayer, and to the ministry of the word."

Work to find balance of prayer and ministry in your life and church.

February

Romans 12:12

"Rejoice in our hope; be patient in tribulation; continue steadfastly in prayer."

Ask for patient endurance and joyful hope in your trials.

February

Romans 15:13

"Now may the God of hope fill you with all joy and peace in believing, that you may abound in hope by the power of the Holy Spirit."

Write your letter to the Holy Spirit and ask for a renewal of hope, joy, and peace in you.

February

1 Corinthians 1:4

"I thank my God always concerning you for the grace of God which was given you by Christ Jesus."

Thank God for one person you are praying for today.

February

1 Corinthians 14:15

"What is it then? I will pray with the spirit, and I will also pray with the understanding. I will sing with the spirit, and I will sing with the understanding also."

Pray both with your heart and with clear thought—ask God to unite spirit and mind.

February

2 Corinthians 1:11

"You also helping together on our behalf by prayer; so that thanks may be given by many persons on our behalf for the gift granted to us by the prayers of many."

Pray for those who serve the gospel and remember to intercede for them.

February

2 Corinthians 12:8–9

"Three times I asked the Lord about this, that it might depart from me. And he said to me, 'My grace is sufficient for you, for my strength is made perfect in weakness.' "

Admit a weakness and ask God to show you grace

February.

Galatians 6:2

"Bear one another's burdens, and so fulfill the law of Christ."

Write a letter to God about someone your life who you are worried about. Ask Him to show you how you can help them bear their burden.

February

Ephesians 1:16–18

*"I don't cease giving thanks for you, making mention of you in
my prayers; that the God of our Lord Jesus Christ, the Father
of glory, may give to you the spirit of wisdom and revelation in
the knowledge of him; the eyes of your understanding being
enlightened..."*

Pray for spiritual insight and wisdom for yourself or someone
you love.

March

Ephesians 3:14–19

"For this cause I bow my knees to the Father of our Lord Jesus Christ… that you may be filled with all the fullness of God."

As you write today, try to open your heart and welcome his love.

March

Ephesians 6:18

"Praying always with all prayer and supplication in the Spirit, and watching thereunto with all perseverance and supplication for all saints."

Consider telling Him about time you've spent with others who have accepted Christ and how you felt while you were with them.

March

Philippians 1:3–4

"I thank my God upon every remembrance of you, always in every prayer of mine making request for you all with joy."

Tell God about someone you've drifted apart from and ask him to be with them today.

March

Philippians 4:6–7

"Don't be anxious about anything, but in everything by prayer and supplication with thanksgiving let your requests be made known to God. And the peace of God, which surpasses all understanding, will guard your hearts and minds through Christ Jesus."

Bring one worry to God along with thanksgiving and receive his peace.

March

Colossians 1:9–12

"We haven't ceased to pray for you, and to desire that you may be filled with the knowledge of his will in all wisdom and spiritual understanding..."

Write to God and ask him to help you accept that his plan may not be the same as his plan for you and that you accept his will in your life.

March

Colossians 4:2

"Continue earnestly in prayer, being vigilant in it with thanksgiving."

Being consistent in the time you pray every day will make it easier to settle into the right frame of mind to write to Him.

March

1 Thessalonians 5:16–18

"Rejoice always. Pray without ceasing. In everything give thanks; for this is the will of God in Christ Jesus concerning you."

Surrender yourself to his plan today. Finish your letter by telling him, :I am here Lord, use me."

March

I designed this to be an occasional devotional, encouraging you to write a letter to God 3 or 4 times a week. But there are three times of the year that I think you should set aside the time to write to God every day. They are special times, Epiphany, Easter and Christmas.

The devotional started in the middle of Epiphany, so Easter is the first opportunity you have to write him every day while you reflect on Christ's crucifixion and resurrection.

Continue writing to God like you are talking to a friend, but for the next 21 days, consider talking to your friend about Jesus' sacrifice to save us from your sins and what accepting him into your life has meant for you.

I understand if writing him every day is a lot and you want to continue your routine of just writing him 3 or 4 letters a week and if that is what you want to do that is perfectly fine. You did buy a book designed to get you stared writing an occasional letter to a friend, not a daily devotional.   The important thing is to do your best to maintain your routine.

Week 1 – Preparing the Heart (Repentance and Reflection)

Joel 2:12–13

"'Yet even now,' says Yahweh, 'turn to me with all your heart, and with fasting, and with weeping, and with mourning.' Tear your heart, and not your garments, and turn to Yahweh, your God; for he is gracious and merciful, slow to anger, and abundant in loving kindness."

Think about a grudge you may be holding, or forgiveness you haven't given and tell God about it. Turn back to him fully and ask him to take your pain.

March 16th

Psalm 51:10

"Create in me a clean heart, O God. Renew a right spirit within me."

Ask God to cleanse and renew your spirit during this season of reflection.

March 17th

Isaiah 1:18

" 'Come now, and let's reason together,' says Yahweh: 'Though your sins be as scarlet, they shall be as white as snow.' "

Thank God for His mercy and his forgiveness of your sins.

March 18th

Matthew 6:6

"But you, when you pray, enter into your inner room, and having shut your door, pray to your Father who is in secret; and your Father who sees in secret will reward you openly."

Find a private place to write your letter. Focus on feeling His presence with you while you write.

March 19th

Matthew 4:4

"But he answered, 'It is written, "Man shall not live by bread alone, but by every word that proceeds out of the mouth of God."'"

Ask God to feed your soul with His Word.

March 20th

James 4:8

"Draw near to God, and he will draw near to you. Cleanse your hands, you sinners, and purify your hearts, you double-minded."

Write to god and invite him to walk by your side. Ask him to forgive your sins and help you be worth of his love.

March 21st

Psalm 139:23–24

"Search me, God, and know my heart. Try me, and know my thoughts. See if there is any wicked way in me, and lead me in the everlasting way."

God knows what is in your heart and mind, but waits patiently for you to come to him. Ask him to help you see what you are denying and ask for his forgiveness.

March 22nd

Week 2 – The Way of the Cross (Sacrifice and Love)

Isaiah 53:5

"But he was pierced for our transgressions. He was crushed for our iniquities. The punishment that brought our peace was on him; and by his wounds we are healed."

Before writing your letter, meditate on Christ's sacrifice for the healing to your soul.

March 23rd

John 1:29

"The next day, he saw Jesus coming to him, and said, 'Behold, the Lamb of God, who takes away the sin of the world!'"

Write a letter to the Lamb thanking him for dying to on the cross to take a way your sins.

March 24th

Matthew 16:24

"Then Jesus said to his disciples, 'If anyone desires to come after me, let him deny himself, and take up his cross, and follow me.'"

Write to God and ask him for the strength to follow the path before you when it seems too hard.

March 25th

Philippians 2:8

"Being found in human form, he humbled himself, becoming obedient to death, yes, the death of the cross."

When you write to the Lord don't boast about your own righteousness like the Pharisees, remain humble in his presence.

March 26th

John 12:24

"Most certainly I tell you, unless a grain of wheat falls into the earth and dies, it remains by itself alone. But if it dies, it bears much fruit."

Ask God to help you surrender what must die so that new life can grow.

March 27th

Luke 22:42

"Saying, 'Father, if you are willing, remove this cup from me. Nevertheless, not my will, but yours, be done.'"

Sometimes you sense gods will, but it seems too costly to do what he asks. Write to him and ask him for the strength to follow the path before you.

March 28th

1 Peter 2:24

"He himself bore our sins in his body on the tree, that we, having died to sins, might live to righteousness; by his wounds you were healed."

Write to Jesus and thank him for bearing your sins. Ask for the strength to live by his example.

March 29th

Week 3 – Resurrection and Renewal (Hope and Victory)

Matthew 28:5–6

"The angel answered the women, 'Don't be afraid, for I know that you seek Jesus, who has been crucified. He is not here, for he has risen, just as he said.'"

Rejoice in the risen Lord and pray to live as one who carries resurrection hope.

March 30th

John 11:25–26

"Jesus said to her, 'I am the resurrection and the life. He who believes in me will still live, even if he dies. Whoever lives and believes in me will never die.'"

Pray to deepen your faith in the eternal life found in Christ alone.

March 31th

Romans 6:4

"We were buried therefore with him through baptism into death, that just like Christ was raised from the dead through the glory of the Father, so we also might walk in newness of life."

Pray to walk daily in the freedom of new life through Christ's resurrection.

April 1stt

Corinthians 15:57

*"But thanks be to God, who gives us the victory through our
Lord Jesus Christ."*

Write to Him and thank him for the sacrifice of his son who died
for our sins.

April 2nd

Colossians 3:1–2

"If then you were raised together with Christ, seek the things that are above, where Christ is, seated at the right hand of God. Set your mind on the things that are above, not on the things that are on the earth."

While you write to Him today remember that your time on earth and material things is temporary and eternal rewards await you in Heaven.

April 3rd

2 Corinthians 5:17

"Therefore if anyone is in Christ, he is a new creation. The old things have passed away. Behold, all things have become new."

Rejoice in your renewal—thank God for making all things new in you.

April 4th

He is Risen!

Revelation 1:17–18

"He laid his right hand on me, saying, 'Don't be afraid. I am the first and the last, and the Living one. I was dead, and behold, I am alive forevermore.'"

Rejoice for today he is Risen. Write to Him about what Jesus' sacrifice on the cross means to you.

April 5th

2 Thessalonians 3:1

"Finally, brethren, pray for us, that the word of the Lord may have free course, and be glorified, even as it is with you."

Think about a way that you can share His Word and ask for the strength to help others find their way to him.

April

1 Timothy 2:1–4

"I exhort therefore, first of all, that supplications, prayers, intercessions, and giving of thanks be made for all men… who will have all men to be saved, and to come to a knowledge of the truth."

When you write to Him today, ask Him to give our leaders wisdom and the strength to do what is write.

April

2 Timothy 1:3

"I thank God, whom I serve with a pure conscience, as my forefathers did, that without ceasing I remember you in my prayers night and day."

While you write your letter today, think about someone who has been your spiritual mentor and thank Him for bringing Him into your life.

April

Titus 3:15

*"All who are with me greet you. Greet those who love us in the
faith. Grace be with you all. Amen."*

Write to Him today and thank him for the community of faith
that supports you're journey with the Lord.

April

Philemon 1:4–6

"I thank my God always, making mention of you in my prayers, hearing of your love and faith which you have toward the Lord Jesus, and toward all the saints; that the fellowship of your faith may become effective in the knowledge of every good thing which is in you in Christ Jesus."

Write to him and ask him to guide your acts of service to align with your faith.

April

Hebrews 4:16

"Let us therefore come boldly to the throne of grace, that we may obtain mercy and find grace to help in time of need."

Write to the Lord and ask him for his mercy and help. He is listening.

April

Hebrews 10:19–22

"Having therefore, brethren, boldness to enter into the holy place by the blood of Jesus… let us draw near with a true heart in full assurance of faith…"

Thank Jesus for opening the way to eternal life and draw nearer to god with a sincere heart.

April

Hebrews 11:6

"But without faith it is impossible to please him: for he that comes to God must believe that he is, and that he is a rewarder of them that diligently seek him."

God is always there for you, all that he requires is your faith. Renew your faith in him today while you talk with your friend.

April

James 1:5

"If any of you lacks wisdom, let him ask of God, who gives to all men liberally and without reproach; and it will be given to him."

If you are struggling with a decision today, ask Him for the wisdom to make the right choice.

April

James 4:2–3

"You lust, and have not. You kill, and desire to have, and cannot obtain: you fight and war. You have not, because you ask not. You ask, and receive not, because you ask amiss..."

Examine your motives in all that you do and ask God to purify your actions.

April

James 4:7–8

"Submit yourselves therefore to God. Resist the devil, and he will flee from you. Draw near to God, and he will draw near to you."

Submit to his will and ask God for the courage and strength to resist temptation.

April

1 Peter 3:12

"For the eyes of the Lord are toward the righteous, and his ears are open to their prayers; but the face of the Lord is against them that do evil."

Take comfort knowing that God listens when you talk to him with sincerity in your heart.

April

1 Peter 4:7

"But the end of all things is at hand: be serious and watchful in your prayers."

Write to him today about what is causing you stress living in our modern times.

April

1 Peter 5:7

"Casting all your care upon him; for he cares for you."

Sometimes it's hard to have faith that he cares about one person out of everyone in the world.   Have faith that he cares and share with Him a specific anxiety today.

April

1 John 1:9

"If we confess our sins, he is faithful and just to forgive us our sins, and to cleanse us from all unrighteousness."

Telling Him that your sin can be scary, but have faith that He loves you and will forgive you if you ask his Grace.

May

1 John 3:22

"And whatever we ask, we receive from him, because we keep his commandments, and do those things that are pleasing in his sight."

Talk to Him today about something that tempts you to sin. Ask him to help you follow the path he has lain before you.

May

1 John 5:14–15

"This is the confidence that we have toward him, that, if we ask anything according to his will, he hears us. And if we know that he hears us, whatever we ask, we know that we have the petitions that we asked of him."

Rest knowing that He is listening when you talk to Him about the times that you have followed His will.

May

Revelation 5:8

"When he had taken the book, the four beasts and four and twenty elders fell down before the Lamb, each one having harps, and golden bowls full of incense, which are the prayers of the saints."

Before writing your letter today, think about worship and then write your words to Him.

May

Psalm 4:1

"Hear me when I call, God of my righteousness! You have relieved me in my distress. Be merciful to me, and hear my prayer."

Call on God to help you with the stress you carry every day and expect his mercy.

May

Psalm 5:3

*"In the morning, LORD, you will hear my voice: in the
morning I will order my prayer to you, and watch."*

Aside from the time you have set aside to write to Him, consider
starting each day with a short mourning prayer. Doing this can
put you in a good frame of mind for the rest of the day.

May

Psalm 17:1

"Hear the right, LORD, attend to my cry, give ear to my prayer, that proceeds not out of deceitful lips."

When you write to him, ask him to guide your heart to day that your actions and intention will be grounded in honesty.

May

Psalm 17:6

"I have called upon you, for you will hear me, O God: incline your ear to me, and hear my speech."

Write to him and be assured, he will hear your words.

May

Psalm 25:16–18

"Turn yourself to me, and have mercy on me; for I am desolate and afflicted. The troubles of my heart are enlarged: O bring me out of my distresses. Look upon my affliction and my pain; and forgive all my sins."

Tell him about your pain, loneliness, and stress and ask him for his mercy and to fill you with his love.

May

Psalm 27:8

"When you said, 'Seek my face,' my heart said to you, 'Your face, LORD, will I seek.' "

Open your heart to God's presence as you write to Him today.

May

Psalm 28:2

*"Hear the voice of my supplications, when I cry to you, when I
lift up my hands toward your holy temple. Selah."*

Today, rather that thinking of praying on bended knee while you
write, think about raising your hands and face to the heavens to
cry out to Him.

May

Psalm 34:4

"I sought the LORD, and he heard me, and delivered me from all my fears."

Write to Him today about a fear and ask Him for the strength to overcome.

May

Psalm 34:17

"The righteous cry, and the LORD hears, and delivers them out of all their troubles."

The Lord has promised that when you pray he will hear and deliver you from your troubles.

May

Psalm 38:9

"All my longings are before you, and my sighing isn't hid from you."

He knows what is deepest in your heart, but He wants to hear it in your own words. Share it with Him today.

May

Psalm 40:1–2

"I waited patiently for the LORD; and he inclined unto me, and heard my cry. He brought me up also out of a horrible pit, out of the miry clay, and set my feet upon a rock, and established my goings."

Tell Him about a time that He helped you find your way out of the darkness and back onto His light.

May

Psalm 50:14

"Offer to God thanksgiving; and pay your vows to the Most High."

When you write to Him today thank Him for all He does and consider renewing vow or commitment you've made.

May

Psalm 51:10–12

"Create in me a clean heart, O God; and renew a right spirit within me... Restore to me the joy of your salvation; and uphold me with your free spirit."

Confess to him your sin without fear, for he will forgive you.

June

Psalm 51:17

"The sacrifices of God are a broken spirit: a broken and a contrite heart, O God, you will not despise."

Humble yourself as you write Him today and ask His comforting presence in your life.

June

Psalm 55:17

"Evening, morning, and at noon I will pray, and cry aloud: and he shall hear my voice."

Aside from writing to Him today, set aside a little extra time for a brief prayer.

June

Psalm 61:1–2

"Hear my cry, O God; attend to my prayer. From the ends of the earth will I cry to you, when my heart is overwhelmed: lead me to the rock that is higher than I."

Tell him about something that is overwhelming you today and ask him for the perspective get through the situation.

June

Psalm 66:19–20

"But certainly God has heard; he has attended to the voice of my prayer. Blessed be God, who has not turned away my prayer, nor his mercy from me."

Write to Him about a time He answered your prayer and thank Him for being faithful to His promise.

June

Psalm 70:1

"Hurry, O God, to deliver me; make haste to help me, O

LORD."

In a time of urgent need, ask Him for His swift guidance.

June

Psalm 84:8–11

"O LORD God of hosts, hear my prayer: give ear, O God of Jacob. Selah… For the LORD God is a sun and shield…"

When you write to Him today ask Him for strength and His blessings.

June

Psalm 86:1–3

"Bow down your ear, O LORD, and hear me: for I am poor and needy. Preserve my soul; for I am holy: O you my God, save your servant… be merciful to me, O Lord: for I cry to you daily."

Be humble when you write to Him today.

June

Psalm 88:1–2

"O LORD God of my salvation, I have cried day and night before you. Let my prayer come before you: incline your ear unto my cry."

Be honest when you tell Him about your sorrows. He is listening.

June

Psalm 94:17

*"Unless the LORD had been my help, my soul had almost dwelt
in silence."*

Thank Him today for a time He lifted you from despair.

June

Psalm 100:4

"Enter into his gates with thanksgiving, and into his courts with praise: be thankful unto him, and bless his name."

Begin your letter with thanks and praise for his presence in your life.

June

Psalm 102:1–2

"Hear my prayer, O LORD, and let my cry come unto you. Don't hide your face from me in the day when I am in trouble..."

Tell him about your troubles today and ask him to remain present in your life,

June

Psalm 102:17

"He will regard the prayer of the destitute, and will not despise their prayer."

Rather than writing about yourself today, write to Him about others in desperate need and lend the weight of your prayers to theirs.

June

Psalm 107:28

"Then they cried unto the LORD in their trouble, and he brought them out of their distresses."

Know that God hears you when you speak to him. He will come to you in your time of need.

June

Psalm 109:4

"For my love they are my adversaries: but I give myself to prayer."

Carrying hatred and anger in your heart only is only hurting yourself. Ask him to help you forgive those who have hurt you and replace your anger with his presence.

June

Psalm 116:1–2

"I love the LORD, because he has heard my voice and my supplications. Because he has inclined his ear unto me, therefore will I call upon him as long as I live."

Renew your promise to talk to Him on a regular basis and continue writing letters to Him.

June

Psalm 118:5

*"I called upon the LORD in distress: the LORD answered me
and set me in a large place."*

Ask the Lord to help you see those around you who need help
and to show you the way to give them aid.

June

Psalm 119:145–146

"I cried with my whole heart; hear me, O LORD: I will keep your statutes. I cried unto you; save me, and I shall keep your testimonies."

Ask Him to help you remain steadfast in your faith as you try to understand His plans for your life.

June

1 Samuel 12:23

"Moreover as for me, far be it from me that I should sin against the LORD by ceasing to pray for you: but I will teach you the good and the right way."

When you write to Him today ask Him for guidance for ways to support your community and share his Word.

July

1 Kings 8:28–30

"Yet give attention to your servant's prayer and his plea for mercy, O LORD my God, and hear the cry and the prayer which your servant prays before you... that your eyes may be open toward this house day and night..."

When you write to him today ask him to help guide your church's outreach to the community.

July

1 Kings 8:49–50

"Then hear thou in heaven their prayer and their supplication, and maintain their cause… that all the peoples of the earth may know the LORD, and fear him."

Write to Him to day about the problems in the world and ask that the leaders of the world hear His word and make decisions that follow His Word.

July

1 Chronicles 16:11

"Seek the LORD and his strength, seek his face continually."

Ask Him to strengthen your faith so that you can follow his Word.

July

2 Chronicles 7:14

"If my people, who are called by my name, shall humble themselves, and pray, and seek my face, and turn from their wicked ways; then will I hear from heaven, and will forgive their sin, and will heal their land."

Be humble in your words when you write to him today and ask Him to help heal your community.

July

Job 22:27

*"You will make your prayer to him, and he will hear you, and
you will pay your vows."*

Before you write to Him today consider any vows you've made
that you haven't followed through on. Ask him for the wisdom
to fulfill one of those vows.

July

Job 42:8

"My servant Job shall pray for you; and I will accept his prayer and I will not deal with you according to your folly; because you have not spoken of me the thing that is right, as my servant Job has."

Focus on humility as you write to Him today and ask for the wisdom to speak clearly when you talk to others about God.

July

A Brief Time of Prayer and Fasting

Because this is an occasional devotional I'm not going to take the time to focus on the summer feasts in the Christian liturgical calendar. There will be plenty of time for that in another edition of Letters to God.

I did, however, want to take a little time during the summer to focus on the power of combining prayer and fasting.

Fasting is mentioned about 77 times in the old and new testament. It is not mentioned to encourage abstinence from food. Fasting is combined with prayer as a spiritual discipline to sharpen your focus and discernment and magnifies your prayers and prepare your heart to accept God. Fasting in the Bible often proceeds breakthrough moments of deliverance, guidance and empowerment.

For instance…

Esther and Israel ~ Esther 4:16 ~ Esther called for three days of fasting before she approached King Xerxes and the result was the salvation of Israel from Haman's plot of genocide.

Nineveh's Salvation ~ Jonah 3:5-10 ~ The people proclaimed a fast and repented, leading God to spare the city from destruction.

Now, I'm not suggesting that you should abstain from eating for 21 days, you need to live your life, but you could practice s modified fast. Perhaps you could practice intermittent fasting ending your fast by writing your letter to God. Or give up something that you do every day. Maybe it is ice cream after dinner or a glass of wine at the end of your work day.

The point is to try to find a connection with God by exercising your personal discipline by denying yourself something that is a part of your daily life.

Daniel 9:3

"Then I set my face unto the Lord God, to seek by prayer and supplications, with fasting, and sackcloth, and ashes."

Consider how turning fully toward God in humility opens the way for His guidance

July 10th

Joel 2:12

"'Yet even now,' says Yahweh, 'turn to me with all your heart, and with fasting, and with weeping, and with mourning.'"

While you are writing your letter today, think about what it means to return wholeheartedly to God without holding back.

July 11th

Ezra 8:23

"So we fasted and begged our God for this: and he granted our request."

Think about the power of combining prayer and fasting when you are seeking God's guidance.

July 12th

Nehemiah 1:4

"When I heard these words, I sat down and wept, and mourned certain days; and I fasted and prayed before the God of heaven."

If you have unresolved grief think about how prayer can bring us closer to God's heart.

July 13th

Esther 4:16

"Go, gather together all the Jews who are in Susa, and fast for me. Don't eat or drink three days, night or day. I and my maidens will also fast in the same way. Then I will go in to the king, which is not according to the law; and if I perish, I perish."

While you are writing to Him today try to find the courage to entrust your life life to his will.

July 14th

Psalm 35:13

"But as for me, when they were sick, my clothing was sackcloth. I afflicted my soul with fasting. My prayer returned into my own bosom."

Before writing to Him think about strengthening your compassion for others through fasting.

July 15th

Isaiah 58:6

"Isn't this the fast that I have chosen: to release the bonds of wickedness, to undo the straps of the yoke, to let the oppressed go free, and that you break every yoke?"

Consider how fasting has been used through out history as a tool in the fight for justice, mercy and to end oppression.

July 16th

Matthew 6:6

"But you, when you pray, enter into your inner room, and having shut your door, pray to your Father who is in secret, and your Father who sees in secret will reward you openly."

As you write to Him today remember that he wants to pray to him with humility rather than standing on the street corner proclaiming how good you righteous you are in your obedience to Him.

July 17th

Matthew 6:16

"Moreover when you fast, don't be like the hypocrites, with sad faces. For they disfigure their faces, that they may be seen by men to be fasting. Most certainly I tell you, they have received their reward."

Just as He prefers humility when you pray, he rewards humility when you fast. Fasting is meant to be done as a devotion to Him, not as a performance to receive approval of others for your piety.

July 18th

Matthew 6:17–18

*"But you, when you fast, anoint your head, and wash your face;
so that you are not seen by men to be fasting, but by your
Father who is in secret, and your Father, who sees in secret,
will reward you."*

While you are fasting, go about your day as you always would.
Don't brag to others about your abstinence, but share it with Him
in when you write your letter.

July 19th

Matthew 17:21

Reflect on the spiritual strength that comes through combining prayer with fasting.

We're now halfway through our fast. While you're thinking about what to write to Him today try to feel your connection to him strengthening through your fast.

July 20th

Mark 9:29

"He said to them, 'This kind can come out by nothing, except by prayer and fasting.'"

Fasting can sharpen your faith and strengthen your spiritual connection to God. Consider this as you write to Him today.

July 21st

Acts 13:3

*"Then, when they had fasted and prayed and laid their hands
on them, they sent them away."*

Before you write your letter today consider how Barnabas and
Saul used fasting to prepare to go on their mission for the church.
Is there a way that your fasting can better prepare you to serve
your community?

July 22nd

Acts 14:23

"When they had appointed elders for them in every assembly, and had prayed with fasting, they commended them to the Lord, on whom they had believed."

If you are participating in the fast now would be a good time to consider how the last two weeks has effected your faith in God. Ask Him for His guidance in everything you do today.

July 23rd

1 Samuel 7:6

"They gathered together to Mizpah, and drew water, and poured it out before Yahweh, and fasted on that day, and said there, 'We have sinned against Yahweh.'"

As you start your third week of fasting remember that fasting is about more than just denial. It is about cleansing yourself and renewing your spiritual bond with God.

July 24rd

2 Chronicles 20:3–4

"Jehoshaphat was afraid, and set himself to seek Yahweh. He proclaimed a fast throughout all Judah. Judah gathered themselves together, to seek help from Yahweh. They came out of all the cities of Judah to seek Yahweh."

While I have reinforced that god likes you to pray and fast in private with him, remember that everyone else who is doing this devotional is fasting with you and throughout the Bible, great things have happened when communities have fasted together.

July 25th

Jonah 3:5

"The people of Nineveh believed God; and they proclaimed a fast, and put on sackcloth, from their greatest even to their least."

Remember that the strength of community fasting saved the people of Nineveh. Don't seek out others to fast with, but know you are part of a community that is strengthening their faith through fasting.

July 26th

Luke 2:37

"She had been a widow for about eighty-four years, who didn't depart from the temple, worshiping with fastings and petitions night and day."

After today, you only have three more days to complete your fast. If you are feeling a your faith growing and your connection to God strengthening consider what occasional fasting could do throughout the year.

July 27th

Luke 4:2

"For forty days he was tempted by the devil. He ate nothing in those days. Afterward, when they were completed, he was hungry."

Before you write your letter today think about how fasting for 40 days strengthened Jesus's spirit and prepared him for victory over Satan's temptations.

July 28th

Acts 10:30

"Cornelius said, 'Four days ago, I was fasting until this hour, and at the ninth hour I prayed in my house, and behold, a man stood before me in bright clothing.'"

Combining fasting and prayer makes you more open to seeing the divine when it comes into your life.

July 29th

Acts 27:33

"While the day was coming on, Paul begged them all to take some food, saying, 'Today is the fourteenth day that you wait and continue fasting, and have taken nothing.'"

Today is the last day of your fast. Take a moment to thank him for his guidance and strength as you have fasted to strengthen your connection with Him.

July 30th

Isaiah 26:3

"You will keep him in perfect peace, whose mind is stayed on you: because he trusts in you."

Write to Him today and ask for His guidance and to help you find an inner peace as you as you make your decisions.

August

Isaiah 30:19

"For the people will dwell in Zion at Jerusalem: you will weep no more: he will surely be gracious to you at the voice of your cry; when he hears, he will answer you."

Write of your fears and stress today. He will hear your words and answer.

August

Jeremiah 17:14

"Heal me, O LORD, and I shall be healed; save me, and I shall be saved: for you are my praise."

Write to him today and talk about your pains and fears and ask him for healing and wisdom.

August

Lamentations 3:22–24

"It is of the LORD's mercies that we are not consumed, because his compassions fail not. They are new every morning: great is your faithfulness. The LORD is my portion, says my soul; therefore will I hope in him."

While you are writing to him today think about the mercies that he has shown you an thank him for his mercy.

August

Joel 2:32

"And it shall come to pass, that whoever shall call on the name of the LORD shall be delivered: for in mount Zion and in Jerusalem there shall be those who shall be saved..."

While you are thinking about what you want to write today think about others who need His grace. Consider asking him to grace those in need with his love today.

August

Micah 7:7

*"But as for me, I will watch for the LORD; I will wait for the
God of my salvation: my God will hear me."*

Write your letter to God today knowing that he will hear your
words, but will reply in his own time.

August

Habakkuk 3:2

"O LORD, I have heard your speech, and was afraid: O LORD, revive your work in the midst of the years, in the midst of the years make it known; in wrath remember mercy."

Renew your relationship with the Lord and reaffirm that you are here to do His will.

August

Proverbs 15:8

"The sacrifice of the wicked is an abomination to the LORD:
but the prayer of the upright is his delight."

As you write to the Lord today tell him about something that is weighting on your heart and ask him to lift you out of the darkness.

August

Proverbs 15:29

"The LORD is far from the wicked: but he hears the prayer of the righteous."

When you write to him today, think about something you feel guilty about and ask his forgiveness. Think about how confessing your sin can bring you closer to God.

August

Proverbs 3:5–6

"Trust in the LORD with all your heart; and lean not unto your own understanding. In all your ways acknowledge him, and he shall direct your paths."

If you have felt lost lately, ask Him to guide your steps back on to the path he has lain before you.

August

Ecclesiastes 5:1–2

"Keep your foot when you go to the house of God: and be more ready to hear than to offer the sacrifice of fools… when you make a vow to God, defer not to pay it…"

As you write your letter today, rather than telling God about what you want to do, listen to what He would like you to do for Him.

August

Matthew 14:23

"And when he had sent the multitudes away, he went up into a mountain apart to pray: and when the evening was come, he was there alone."

Try to set aside a solitary time each day when you write your letter to God.

August

Matthew 26:36–44

"My Father, if it is possible, let this cup pass from me:
nevertheless not as I will, but as you will."

When you are facing things that feel overwhelming it is easy to feel like He has forsaken you. Write to Him today about your challenges and trust that He is still by your side.

August

Mark 1:35

"And in the morning, rising up a great while before day, he went out, and departed into a solitary place, and there prayed."

Try writing your letter at different times each day. Is there a time when you feel it Is easier to her His voice? If so, consider changing the time you write to him each day.

August

Luke 1:13–20

"Your petition is heard; and your wife Elisabeth shall bear you a son..."

Know that He hears your words and is capable of granting incredible blessings!

August

Luke 1:46–55

"My soul magnifies the Lord, and my spirit has rejoiced in God my Savior."

When you write today, take a little time to offer thanks for all that he has done.

August

"My soul magnifies the Lord, and my spirit has rejoiced in God my Savior."

Luke 6:12

"In these days he went out into the mountain to pray, and continued all night in prayer to God."

Today, consider setting aside extra time to sit quietly in contemplation and silent prayer.

August

Luke 22:41–44

"He was withdrawn from them about a stone's cast, and kneeled down and prayed, saying, Father, if you are willing, remove this cup from me: nevertheless not my will, but yours, be done."

When you are feeling overwhelmed, open your heart to him and seek his grace as your guide.

September

Acts 1:14

"These all continued with one accord in prayer and supplication, with the women, and Mary the mother of Jesus, and with his brothers."

Writing letters to God is a great way to build a habit of regular prayer, but it is a solitary practice. Consider joining a prayer group to commune with the Lord as a group.

September

Acts 12:5–12

"Peter was kept in prison: but prayer was made without ceasing of the church unto God for him."

Think about people in your life who could use his grace today, write to Him and ask him to be with them today.

September

Acts 16:25

"About midnight, Paul and Silas prayed, and sang praises unto God: and the prisoners heard them."

Our lives can become so busy that something as simple as taking ten minutes to pray can seem like too much. Regular prayer, (writing your to your friend) can become a stabilizing anchor in your life.

September

Acts 20:36

"When he had thus spoken, he kneeled down, and prayed with them all."

Writing to God on a regular basis helps to keep your faith focused, but he wants more than that. Consider helping to spread his word by setting an example in your life. The next time you are out at dinner, take a moment to pray before starting your meal.

September

Romans 8:26–27

"Likewise the Spirit also helps our infirmities: for we know not what we should pray for as we ought: but the Spirit himself makes intercession for us with groanings which cannot be uttered."

If you are having trouble deciding what to write today, try opening your heart to the Holy Spirit and let him inspire your words.

September

1 Corinthians 7:5

"He who speaks in an unknown tongue speaks not to men, but to God: for no man understands him… he speaks mysteries by the Spirit."

Write to Him today and ask him to help your religious leaders find clarity and strengthen their connection to Him.

September

2 Corinthians 9:14

"While by their prayer for you they long after you because of the exceeding grace of God in you."

While you write to him today consider what you could do that will help others see his grace through your actions.

September

Philippians 1:3–11

"I thank my God upon every remembrance of you... being confident of this very thing, that he who began a good work in you will perform it until the day of Jesus Christ."

Ask him to guide your steps today so you can continue do the work he has planned for you.

October

1 Thessalonians 3:10

"That we might see you face to face, and might perfect that which is lacking in your faith?"

When you write to him today, ask him to give you the strength to help others find their way to join you in your faith.

October

2 Thessalonians 1:11

"Wherefore also we pray always for you, that our God would count you worthy of this calling, and fulfill all the good pleasure of his goodness and the work of faith with power."

Put your faith in Him that He has a plan for you and through your faith, He will help you see his presence in your life.

October

Matthew 18:19–20

"Again I say unto you, That if two of you shall agree on earth as touching anything that they shall ask, it shall be done for them of my Father which is in heaven. For where two or three are gathered together in my name, there am I in the midst of them."

Don't remain solitary in your faith. Make time to attend church and/or join a prayer group.   Joining others of faith with strengthen and grow your own.

October

Mark 11:24

"Therefore I tell you, whatever things you desire, when you pray, believe that you receive them, and you will have them."

If you are struggling with your faith today, write and ask Him to help you see the times He has been present in your life.

October

Acts 4:31

"And when they had prayed, the place was shaken where they had assembled together; and they were all filled with the Holy Spirit."

While you write your letter today, open yourself to be filled with the Holy Spirit.

October

Romans 15:30

"Now I beg you, brethren, for the Lord Jesus Christ's sake, and for the love of the Spirit, that you strive together with me in your prayers to God for me."

When you write your letter today, consider asking Him to guide you to others who can work with you on the path He has prepared for you.

October

Philippians 4:19

"But my God shall supply all your need according to his riches in glory by Christ Jesus."

Rather than telling Him what you want, ask him to provide what He knows you need.

October

Colossians 4:12

"Epaphras, who is one of you, a bondservant of Christ, saluteth you, always laboring fervently for you in prayers..."

We all have people in our lives who have our best interests at heart. Thank Him today for putting those people in your life.

October

James 5:16

"Confess your faults one to another, and pray for one another, that you may be healed. The effectual fervent prayer of a righteous man avails much."

Don't be afraid to share your faults with him. He understands we are mortal and will make mistakes. All he wants is your honesty and an honest effort to try to do better.

October

Psalm 91:1–2

"He that dwells in the secret place of the Most High shall abide under the shadow of the Almighty... He is my refuge and my fortress: my God; in him will I trust."

If you're felling lost or vulnerable today, ask him to shelter you with his love.

October

Isaiah 40:28–31

"Hast you not known? Have you not heard that the everlasting God, the LORD, the Creator of the ends of the earth... they that wait upon the LORD shall renew their strength..."

Think today about times when you have had more inner strength than you thought while you have been serving Him. Thank Him for always being by your side.

October

Jeremiah 33:3

"Call unto me, and I will answer you, and show you great and mighty things, which you know not."

When you are talking with your friend today, ask Him to show you something within you that you are denying is there.

October

Daniel 6:10

"Now when Daniel knew that the writing was signed, he went into his house; and his windows being open in his chamber toward Jerusalem, he kneeled upon his knees three times a day, and prayed, and gave thanks before his God, as he did aforetime."

This is an occasional devotional, designed to make it easy for you to start praying on a regular basis. Now is a good time to consider adopting a daily time to write to your friend.

October

Habakkuk 2:1

"I will stand post, and watch in the watchtower, and will look to see what he will say unto me, and what I will answer when I am reproved."

When you write to Him today, reaffirm that you are here to serve His needs. Try keeping it simple, "I am here Lord, use me." Now take a little time to sit quietly and listen for His words.

October

Zechariah 8:21–23

"And many people and strong nations shall come to seek the LORD of hosts in Jerusalem, and to pray before the LORD."

Write to your friend today and ask Him to guide the worlds leaders to seek His wisdom when they are making decisions that effect nations.

October

International Day of Prayer for the Persecuted

Matthew 5:10

"Blessed are those who have been persecuted for righteousness' sake, for theirs is the Kingdom of Heaven."

When talk to your friend today ask him to share his love and protection with Christians around the globe who are being targeted for their Christian Faith. Ask Him to share His strength with them so they can continue to stand strong in their faith.

November 1st

Malachi 1:11

"For from the rising of the sun even to its going down my name shall be great among the nations; and in every place incense shall be offered unto my name, and a pure offering..."

While you're talking to Him today ask Him for his guidance to find a way that you can help the global Christian community.

November

Ruth 1:16–17

*"Whither you go, I will go; and where you lodge, I will lodge...
The LORD do so to me, and more also, if even death parts me
and you."*

When you write to Him today, recommit your faith and ask Him
to be with those you love.

November

Haggai 1:5–7(163)

"Consider your ways… Is it time for you, O you, to dwell in your paneled houses, and this house to lie waste?"

Ask him today to for wisdom and to help you understand where your priorities should lye.

November

Jonah 2:7–9

"When my soul fainted within me I remembered the LORD: and my prayer came in unto you, into your holy temple... Salvation is of the LORD."

When you write to Him today, consider telling him about a recent moment when your faith wavered and ask for his salvation.

November

Ezra 8:21–23

"There by the river Ahava I proclaimed a fast… that we might humble ourselves before our God, to seek of him a right way for us…"

When you are talking to a friend, don't be afraid to ask for His guidance as you make your decisions today.

November

Psalm 30:4–5

"Sing praise to the LORD, O you saints of his, and give thanks at the remembrance of his holiness. For his anger endures but a moment; in his favor is life: weeping may endure for a night, but joy comes in the morning."

While you may feel doubt and fear in the darkness of the night, take a moment to enjoy the sun of the morning and feel joy at remembering the promises He has kept.

November

Psalm 42:1–2

"As the deer pants for the water brooks, so pants my soul after you, O God. My soul thirsts for God, for the living God..."

Just as our bodies need water to survive, our soul needs gods love to thrive. Open yourself to accept his love today.

November

Isaiah 65:24

"It shall come to pass, that before they call, I will answer; and while they are yet speaking, I will hear."

Some days it is hard to put our thoughts in to words, much less write them down. Remember that He already knows what you need and will know your heart regardless of what you say.

November

Micah 6:8

"He has shown you, O man, what is good; and what does the LORD require of you, but to do justly, and to love mercy, and to walk humbly with your God?"

When you write to Him today, ask for the strength and humility to give others grace when your frustrated with them.

November

Zephaniah 3:17

"The LORD your God in the midst of you is mighty; he will save, he will rejoice over you with joy; he will rest in his love, he will joy over you with singing."

Always know that He loves you and celebrates in joy with you when you embrace your faith.

November

Malachi 3:16

"Then they that feared the LORD spoke often one to another: and the LORD listened, and heard it, and a book of remembrance was written before him for them that feared the LORD, and that thought upon his name."

If you are struggling with your faith, find others to pray with and share your stories of the times that you have seen His hand in your life..

November

Luke 6:12

*"In these days he went out into the mountain to pray, and
continued all night in prayer to God."*

Consider taking a little time for reflection and meditation before
writing to your friend each day.

November

Hebrews 13:15

"By him therefore let us offer the sacrifice of praise to God continually, that is, the fruit of our lips giving thanks to his name."

Remember to offer Him thanks throughout your day for the moments when you can see His presence in your life.

November

1 Thessalonians 5:25

"Brethren, pray for us."

It's easy to forget that prayers can be short and simple. When you write to Him today remember that you are writing to a friend and you don't have to be formal or stand on ceremony.

November

3 John 1:2

"Beloved, I wish above all things that you may prosper and be in health, even as your soul prospers."

A regular routine of prayer has proven health benefits. Make writing your letters to Him a regular part of your life.

November

Advent

Today we being the Advent season. For the next 25 day we will begin preparing to celebrate the birth of Christ!

For so many this time of year begins the mad dash through the holiday season. Cleaning, getting ready for guests, preparing meals, shopping, there is never enough time.

It may be cliche, but it's important to remember why we celebrate Christmas.

During the Advent season and through Epiphany on Jan 6th, I'm suggesting you take time everyday to write a letter to the Lord. Use this time each day to slow down and reflect on what the birth of the Lord has meant to the world.

 As you progress through the Advent season, take a moment each day to prepare your heart to accept the love of the Lord when we celebrate the birth of the Son.

Hope in Promise

Isaiah 7:14

"Therefore the Lord himself will give you a sign. Behold, the virgin will conceive, and bear a son, and shall call his name Immanuel."

When you write to Him today, tell him what accepting Jesus into your heart has meant for you.

December 1st

Isaiah 9:6

"For a child is born to us. A son is given to us; and the government will be on his shoulders. His name will be called Wonderful Counselor, Mighty God, Everlasting Father, Prince of Peace."

Take a moment to thank Him for the sacrifice of his only begotten Son.

December 2nd

Isaiah 11:1

"A shoot will come out of the stock of Jesse, and a branch out of his roots will bear fruit."

Let the birth of Christ be a time to renew your relationship with God and strengthen your faith.

December 3rd

Isaiah 40:3

"The voice of one who calls out, 'Prepare the way of Yahweh in the wilderness. Make a level highway in the desert for our God.'"

Ask Him to help you stay focused on preparing to welcome Christ into your heart during this hectic time.

December 4th

Isaiah 40:5

"Then Yahweh's glory will be revealed, and all flesh will see it together; for the mouth of Yahweh has spoken it."

As you go through your day watch for his presence in your life and in the lives of those around you.

December 5th

Preparation and Expectation

Micah 5:2

"But you, Bethlehem Ephrathah, being small among the clans of Judah, out of you one will come out to me who is to be ruler in Israel; whose goings out are from of old, from ancient times."

Consider today that Gods greatest work didn't enter the world in a grand moment, but in a humble location. Are you open to His sublte actions in your life.

December 6th

Malachi 3:1

"Behold, I send my messenger, and he will prepare the way before me! The Lord, whom you seek, will suddenly come to his temple."

It is hard to see His actions in your life when they are happening. Ask Him for the wisdom to see His presence in the world during Advent.

December 7th

Zechariah 9:9

"Rejoice greatly, daughter of Zion! Shout, daughter of Jerusalem! Behold, your King comes to you! He is righteous, and having salvation; lowly, and riding on a donkey."

Jesus came into the world in the humble setting of manger in Bethlehem. Remember during the Advent to give grace to those around you and be humble before the lord.

December 8th

Zechariah 12:10

"I will pour on the house of David, and on the inhabitants of Jerusalem, the spirit of grace and of supplications."

Ask the Holy Spirit to fill you with His grace as you open your heart to prepare for the coming of the Lord.

December 9th

Matthew 1:21

*"She shall give birth to a son. You shall call his name Jesus,
for it is he who shall save his people from their sins."*

When you write to Him, thank Him for forgiving your sins and
ask Him to help you find a fresh start in the new year.

December 10th

Joy in the Announcement

Luke 1:28

"Having come in, the angel said to her, 'Rejoice, you highly favored one! The Lord is with you. Blessed are you among women!'"

Ask Him to help you understand when His call comes so that you will be prepared to do what he asks.

December 11th

Luke 1:30–31

"Then the angel said to her, 'Don't be afraid, Mary; for you have found favor with God. Behold, you will conceive in your womb, and bring forth a son; and you shall call his name Jesus.'"

Ask him to fill you with peace when you are afraid to take the actions he has asked of you.

December 12th

Luke 1:46–47

"Mary said, 'My soul magnifies the Lord, and my spirit has rejoiced in God my Savior.'"

Thank about what you can do today that will magnify the Lord's love in the world.

December 13th

Luke 1:76–79

"You, child, will be called a prophet of the Most High; for you will go before the face of the Lord to prepare his ways, to give knowledge of salvation to his people by the remission of their sins, because of the tender mercy of our God, whereby the dawn from on high will visit us."

We're past the half way point of the Advent. Take time to ask Him for forgiveness of any sins you've hidden even from yourself.

December 14th

Luke 2:7

"She gave birth to her firstborn son. She wrapped him in swaddling cloths, and laid him in a manger; because there was no room for them in the inn."

Think about the humble surroundings of Jesus' birth and ask Him today to show you a way to honor Jesus in simple ways.

December 15th

Love in the Coming of Christ

Luke 2:10–11

"The angel said to them, 'Don't be afraid; for behold, I bring you good news of great joy, which will be to all the people. For to you is born this day in the city of David a Savior, who is Christ the Lord.'"

Tell Him about the joy you have experienced since you have opened your heart to Him.

December 16th

Matthew 1:23

"Behold, the virgin shall be with child, and shall bring forth a son. They shall call his name Immanuel; which is, being interpreted, 'God with us.'"

Thank Him today for His steady presence in your life.

December 17th

Psalm 72:10–11

"The kings of Tarshish and of the islands will bring tribute. The kings of Sheba and Seba will offer gifts. Yes, all kings shall fall down before him. All nations shall serve him."

Think today about something you can do to help others without expectation of their returning the favor or even giving you their thanks. This is the gift you can give to others this Advent season.

December 18th

Isaiah 60:1

"Arise, shine; for your light has come, and Yahweh's glory has risen on you."

When you talk with Him today, tell him about yow you are reflecting Christ's light in your home and relationships during the holiday season.

December 19th

Isaiah 64:1

"Oh that you would tear the heavens, that you would come down, that the mountains might quake at your presence."

It is easy to feel overwhelmed by His presence, but He loves you and wants to fill your heart with hope. Talk to Him today about an area in your life that feels broken and ask Him to fill that part of your life with His love.

December 20th

Christ Our Redeemer and Hope
Romans 13:11–12

"Knowing the time, that it is already the hour for you to wake out of sleep; for now salvation is nearer to us than when we first believed."

Write to Him today and ask Him to help you prepare to welcome Christ's light into the world.

December 21st

Galatians 4:4–5

"But when the fullness of the time came, God sent out his Son, born to a woman, born under the law, that he might redeem those who were under the law, that we might receive the adoption of children."

Take time while your writing to your friend today to thank Him for sending his son to redeem us and open the path to heaven.

December 22nd

Philippians 4:4–5

"Rejoice in the Lord always! Again I will say, Rejoice! Let your gentleness be known to all men. The Lord is at hand."

Christ is near, ask Him today to show you how to share the gentleness of Christ with others.

December 23rd

Titus 2:11–13

"For the grace of God has appeared, bringing salvation to all men, instructing us to live soberly, righteously, and godly in this present world; looking for the blessed hope and appearing of the glory of our great God and Savior, Jesus Christ."

Ask Him to share with you the grace of Christs coming into the world.

December 24th

Revelation 22:20

"He who testifies these things says, 'Yes, I come quickly.'
Amen! Come, Lord Jesus."

End your Advent today by thanking him for birth of the Lord Jesus!

December 25th

As we finish Advent and finish out the year, I'm continuing to encourage you to write a daily letter to God. It would be easy to let the celebration of Christ's birth be the culmination of our prayers for the year. To sit back and maybe take the time between Christmas and New Years to put our feet up and catch up on some rest.

This isn't the end of the special season though. For many around the world, it is the start of the build up to the Epiphany! It the west the Epiphany celebrates the arrival of the Magi celebrating the birth of Jesus as King.

It the east, the Epiphany is focused on Christ's baptism and first miracle. It highlights His Divinity and marks the beginning of his public ministry, symbolizing light overcoming darkness.

If you ever want to see the joy of the Epiphany, spend some time on Google watching young men in Greece diving in to the water to retrieve the Cross.

Because the build up to Epiphany, in my opinion, begins the day after Christmas and runs up to Jan 6th, this part of Letters to God will be broken up between the 2026 and 2027 editions of Letters to God.

It is, of course, my hope that you have already purchased the 2027 addition of Letters to God, or that I have inspired you to take the step to a daily devotional and have purchased the 2027 version of Letters to God: 365 Letters of Faith, Hope and Gratitude.

Either way, lets try to keep the daily letters to god going for the last week of the year.

The Word Became Flesh

John 1:14

"The Word became flesh and lived among us. We saw his glory, such glory as of the one and only Son of the Father, full of grace and truth."

Before you Write to Him today think about where you've seen God's grace in your life or those around you. Ask Him to help you see his presence around you.

December 26th

Light Shines in the Darkness

John 1:5

"The light shines in the darkness, and the darkness hasn't overcome it."

Are you struggling with fear or confusion as the year is coming to an end? Ask Him to shine the light of his love into your life.

December 27th

A Child Is Given

Isaiah 11:2

"The Spirit of Yahweh will rest on him: the spirit of wisdom and understanding, the spirit of counsel and might, the spirit of knowledge and of the fear of Yahweh."

Thank Him today for his for His wisdom and counsel. And most importantly, his understanding.

December 28th

God With Us

Matthew 1:23

"'Behold, the virgin shall be with child, and shall give birth to a son. They shall call his name Immanuel,' which is interpreted, 'God with us.'"

Remember that He is always with you. If you are struggling with what to say today, talk about what is in your heart. He knows what you are really trying to say.

December 29th

Glory to God in the Highest

Luke 2:14

"'Glory to God in the highest, on earth peace, good will toward men.'"

Today, write Him about a moment in your life when you shared the glory of God with others.

December 30th

We Have Seen His Salvation

Luke 2:30–32

"For my eyes have seen your salvation… a light for revelation to the nations, and the glory of your people Israel."

Today we celebrate the baptism of Jesus. Think about how Jesus has brought His light into your life and ask God for a renewed understanding of His glory.

December 31st

Thank you for joining me on my journey of faith. Despite my age, I am very new to accepting Jesus into my heart, and I understand the challenges of establishing a daily prayer routine. I hope that using this book has helped you grow in your own faith and deepen your relationship with God.

I know the 2026 edition of this book—and my daily devotional— were released after the first of the year, but God did not move me to create it until late in 2025. Going forward, my goal is to write annual editions of Letters to God. I would truly love for you to continue writing your own letters to God as a way to build your faith and welcome His grace more fully into your life.

If this devotional has left you feeling ready for more, I invite you to look for my daily devotional, Letters to God: 365 Letters of Faith, Hope, and Gratitude.

Thank you again for supporting my work.

Made in the USA
Monee, IL
07 July 2026

56546409R00134